# YOU BELONG TO FAMILIES
## HISTORY & GEOGRAPHY 105

Introduction |1

1. **Morning** .................................................................... 2
   Getting Ready |2
   Learning about Maps |6
   Walking to School |8
   Self Test 1 |11

2. **The School Family** ................................................ 12
   Classmates and Teachers |14
   More Family Members |16
   All Day with Jesus |20
   Self Test 2 |22

3. **God's Church Family** ........................................... 23
   My Pastor |24
   More Family Members |26
   Our Worship of God |28
   Self Test 3 |32

   LIFEPAC Test |**Pull-out at the back of the booklet**

804 N. 2nd Ave. E.
Rock Rapids, IA 51246-1759

© MCMXCVI by Alpha Omega Publications, Inc. All rights reserved. LIFEPAC is a registered trademark of Alpha Omega Publications, Inc.

All trademarks and/or service marks referenced in this material are the property of their respective owners. Alpha Omega Publications, Inc. makes no claim of ownership to any trademarks and/or service marks other than their own and their affiliates, and makes no claim of affiliation to any companies whose trademarks may be listed in this material, other than their own.

**Author:**
Kathleen McNaughton

**Editor:**
Mary Ellen Quint, M.A.

**Consulting Editor:**
Howard Stitt, Th.M., Ed.D.

**Revision Editor:**
Alan Christopherson, M.S.

**Media Credits:**
Page 17, 31: © bluebearry, iStock, Thinkstock;
28: © 168stock, iStock, Thinkstock.

# YOU BELONG TO FAMILIES | Unit 5

## Learn with our friends!

When you see me, I will help your teacher explain the exciting things you are expected to do.

When you do actions with me, you will learn how to write, draw, match words, read, and much more.

You and I will learn about matching words, listening, drawing, and other fun things in your lessons.

Follow me and I will show you new, exciting truths that will help you learn and understand what you study. Let's learn!

Unit 5 | **YOU BELONG TO FAMILIES**

# YOU BELONG TO FAMILIES

I'm Bobby! This picture shows my school and my church. On Sunday, I go to church to worship God. I am going to tell you all about my school and my church.

## Objectives

**Read these objectives.** They will tell what you will be able to do when you have finished this LIFEPAC®.

1. I can tell the name of my school and my church.
2. I can tell about the school family.
3. I can tell about God's church family.

YOU BELONG TO FAMILIES | Unit 5

# 1. MORNING

Morning is here already.
My clock says, "Wake up!"
I hear Mother calling.
I must get ready for school.

# Getting Ready

The first thing I do is open the curtains.
What kind of day is today?
The weather helps me know what to wear.
Mother calls, "Breakfast is ready."
A good breakfast is important.
It will give me energy to work and play.

Unit 5 | **YOU BELONG TO FAMILIES**

 Write *1*, *2*, and *3* to show what happens *first*, *second*, and *third*.

Match the clothes to the weather.

Section 1 | **3**

# YOU BELONG TO FAMILIES | Unit 5

 Color the picture of the person who had a good breakfast.

 Draw what you had for breakfast.

 Circle *yes* or *no*.

Did you have a good breakfast?

yes    no

Unit 5 | **YOU BELONG TO FAMILIES**

 Color the picture and talk about it.

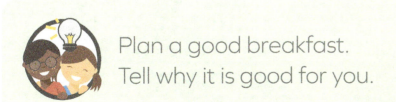 Plan a good breakfast.
Tell why it is good for you.

YOU BELONG TO FAMILIES | Unit 5

# Learning about Maps

Here comes my friend, Jimmy.
Jimmy and I walk to school.

This picture is a map.
It shows where my school is.

Can you find Jimmy's house?
Can you find Bobby's house?
Where is the school?

**Draw a map of your classroom.**

Show where all the desks are.
Show the windows and the doors.

Remember: A map is a picture that shows how something looks from above.

# Walking to School

"I'm all ready, Jimmy. Let's go!" says Bobby.
"We can walk through the park today.
Maybe we'll see Police Officer Lopez."

Bobby and Jimmy are careful crossing streets.
They look both ways.
Then, they walk across the street.
At the stoplight, they wait for the light to say "walk."

Unit 5 | **YOU BELONG TO FAMILIES**

 **Write the answers to these questions in your writing tablet.**

What is your name?

What is the name of your school?

How old are you?

How many years have you been in school?

 **In your writing tablet, tell how you get to school.**

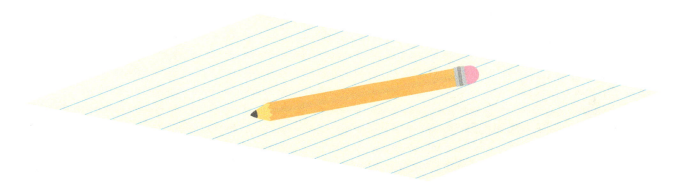

YOU BELONG TO FAMILIES | Unit 5

## Finding Things on a Map

 Listen and do.

 Draw a red line from Bobby and Jimmy to Police Officer Lopez.

 **Before you take the Self Test, study what you have read and done.** The Self Test will check what you remember.

Unit 5 | **YOU BELONG TO FAMILIES**

# SELF TEST 1

**Each answer =** 1 point

**Circle *yes* or *no*.**

Bobby eats a good breakfast.
yes          no

A good breakfast makes you sleepy.
yes          no

Maps tell us how to get from place to place.
yes          no

Run to cross the street in a hurry.
yes          no

**Match the picture with its name.**

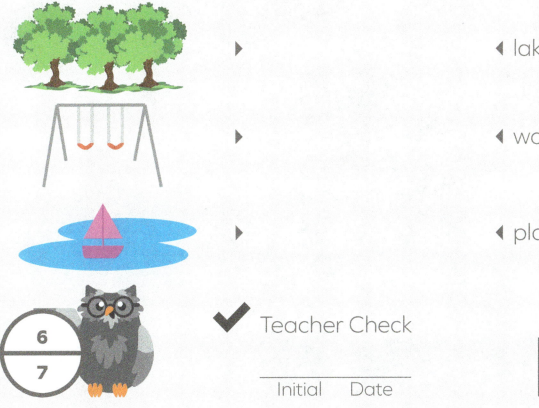

◀ lake

◀ woods

◀ playground

✓ Teacher Check

_____
Initial   Date

My Score

Section 1 | **11**

## 2. THE SCHOOL FAMILY

Bobby and Jimmy are part of the school family.
Their teacher and principal are part of the school family.
Their classmates are part of the school family, too.

Can you think of others who are part of the school family?

Unit 5 | **YOU BELONG TO FAMILIES**

Draw a picture of your school.

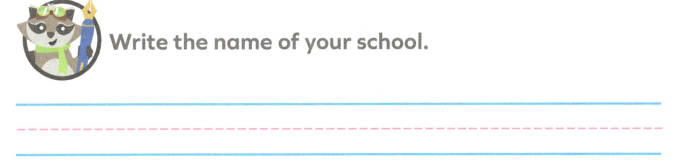

Write the name of your school.

# Classmates and Teachers

My classmates are my friends.
We are part of the school family.
Families love and help each other.

We are kind to one another as we play together at recess.
We help each other with lessons.
In these ways, we show our love for each other.

Unit 5 | **YOU BELONG TO FAMILIES**

My teacher is Mr. James.
He helps us learn new things.
He teaches us God's Word.
Mr. James works with us all day.

 Follow the dots.

Section 2 | 15

# More Family Members

God has put other helpers in my school.
Mr. Howard is our principal.
He is a good friend.
He makes sure everything goes well at school.

Mr. Riley keeps our school clean.
I help him by picking up litter in school and on the playground.

Unit 5 | **YOU BELONG TO FAMILIES**

Mrs. Wills is the school secretary. She helps make sure that every day in our school is a good one.

I should thank God each day for all the members of my school family.

 **Draw a picture of your school family.**

# YOU BELONG TO FAMILIES | Unit 5

 **Circle persons who are part of the school family.**

| | | |
|---|---|---|
| mother | teacher | grandpa |
| secretary | father | firefighter |
| classmates | principal | Mr. Riley |

 **Draw lines from the words to the pictures.**

Mr. Riley ▶

mother ▶

teacher ▶

classmates ▶

Unit 5 | **YOU BELONG TO FAMILIES**

 Color the pictures.

YOU BELONG TO FAMILIES | Unit 5

# All Day with Jesus

Going to school is very important.
You want to do your best.
You need Jesus to help you in your classroom.
You need Jesus to help you when you play at recess.
Jesus helps you do and say the right things all day long.

Unit 5 | **YOU BELONG TO FAMILIES**

**Circle the right word.**

A _____ teaches you math.
( teacher / firefighter )

School is a place to work and _____ .
( play / sleep )

Jesus helps us do our _____ .
( worst / best )

 **Put a line under all the children who are listening to Jesus.**

 **Before you take the Self Test, study what you have read and done.** The Self Test will check what you remember.

YOU BELONG TO FAMILIES | Unit 5

# SELF TEST 2

**Each answer =** 1 point

**Draw lines to the right people.**

He keeps our
school clean.      ▶                    ◀ Jimmy and Bobby

They walk
to school.         ▶                    ◀ Mr. James

He teaches
Bobby to read.     ▶                    ◀ Mr. Riley

**Circle the children who are walking with Jesus.**

Teacher Check

_____
Initial    Date

My Score

Unit 5 | **YOU BELONG TO FAMILIES**

# 3. GOD'S CHURCH FAMILY

A church family is called a congregation.
The congregation worships God.
Bobby belongs to this family.
Pastor Johnson leads the congregation.
Other people help care
for the church family.

# My Pastor

This is a picture of my church.
Jimmy and I belong to this church.

Pastor Johnson is our friend. He loves God and God's people. He shows his love by telling people about Jesus.

Unit 5 | **YOU BELONG TO FAMILIES**

 **Learn this verse.**

"For God so loved the world,
that He gave His only begotten Son,
that whosoever believeth in Him should not perish,
but have everlasting life."  (John 3:16)

 **Draw a picture of your church.**

 **Write the name of your church.**

Section 3 | **25**

# More Family Members

Our church family has many members.
Church members help the janitor keep the church neat and clean.
Some members work in the office.
Some members help our pastor teach the word of God.

Unit 5 | **YOU BELONG TO FAMILIES**

 **Circle the things people can do to help in church.**

 **Circle the right word.**

A church family is called a _____.
( house / congregation )

The _____ leads the congregation.
( pastor / teacher )

# Our Worship of God

God says our church is a house of prayer.
He wants His people to come together.
We go to church to worship God.
We worship in prayer and song.
We show our love for God when we worship in His house.
We worship God in many ways.

Unit 5 | **YOU BELONG TO FAMILIES**

 Circle each person you see who is worshipping.

Section 3 | **29**

# YOU BELONG TO FAMILIES | Unit 5

**Draw a picture of something you can do to help others in your church.**

Unit 5 | **YOU BELONG TO FAMILIES**

# Which Family?

 Circle the right word.

church / home

home / school

school / home

school / home

church / school

church / home

 **Before you take the Self Test, study what you have read and done.** The Self Test will check what you remember.

# SELF TEST 3

**Each answer =** 1 point

**Circle *yes* or *no*.**

You belong to a school family.

yes        no

You work and play in church.

yes        no

You worship God when you pray.

yes        no

**Draw a line to the right person.**

This person leads
the church family. ▶

This person teaches
God's Word. ▶

✓ Teacher Check

_____
Initial    Date

My Score

Unit 5 | **YOU BELONG TO FAMILIES**

# Take Home Activity — Hidden Pictures

**Find these things hidden in the big picture:** whale, thimble, thread, shell, ship, chimpanzee.

Unit 105 | **HISTORY & GEOGRAPHY**

# HISTORY & GEOGRAPHY 105
## LIFEPAC TEST

Name _____

Date _____

My Score

# HISTORY & GEOGRAPHY 105: LIFEPAC TEST

**Each answer =** 1 point

**Circle the right word.**

Eating a good breakfast is _____ .
( good / bad )

Bobby and Jimmy _____ to school.
( ride / walk )

_____ tell us how to get from one place to another.
( Cars / Maps )

Your family has _____ member.
( one / more than one )

**Circle the right words.**

church family

home family

church family

school family

Unit 105 | **HISTORY & GEOGRAPHY**

# Match the picture and the words.

   ◀ school

   ◀ church

   ◀ home

# HISTORY & GEOGRAPHY | Unit 105